JavaScript Professional Programming Made Easy

By Sam Key

Expert JavaScripts Programming Language Success in a Day for Any Computer User!

Table Of Contents

Introduction

I want to thank you and congratulate you for purchasing the book, "Professional JavaScript Programming Made Easy: Expert JavaScripts Programming Language Success In A Day for Any Computer User!"

This book contains proven steps and strategies on how to code JavaScript from scratch.

This book will give you a solid idea on how JavaScript works and how it can be applied to your web pages. This is an ideal book that every beginner should read. However, it is required that you already know HTML and CSS.

Familiarity with other programming languages such as Java, Visual Basic, and C is a plus since it will make it easier for you to learn and understand the concepts behind the processes involved in coding JavaScript.

Every explanation in the book will be accompanied by an example. Those examples will be shown in Courier New font; in case that font is not available, it will be shown in a monospaced generic family font instead.

To learn and code JavaScript, all you need is a text editing tool such as Notepad in Windows or TextEdit in Macintosh computers. However, it is recommend that you use a source code editor or a text editing tool with syntax highlighting that supports HTML, CSS, and JavaScript languages to speed up your learning and reduce the typos you will make.

One of the best and free source code editor tools you can get from the internet is Notepad++. It will be discussed in the last chapter of the book.

Thanks again for purchasing this book, I hope you enjoy it!

Chapter 1: Introduction to JavaScript

JavaScript is a scripting or programming language that is mainly used for web pages. Almost all websites use it to provide their visitors a richer browsing experience. Compared to coding HTML, JavaScript is real programming.

It is safe to say that JavaScript is the most popular and most widely used programming language in the world. JavaScript is easy to learn, and that is why web developers or even hobbyists can use it after a few days of studying it.

Unlike other programming languages, JavaScript is easy to learn and apply practically. The programs or scripts created from JavaScript are used by millions of people – even though they do not know they are already using them.

JavaScript can turn your old HTML files, which are static, into dynamic. You can embed JavaScript into your files for you to deliver web pages with dynamic content and appearance.

To embed JavaScript to your HTML file, you must enclose your script inside script HTML tags (<script></script>). Commonly, you should place the script tags inside the head HTML tags (<head></head>). However, there will be times that you might want or need to place them inside your page's body (<body></body>).

On the other hand, JavaScript can be placed in an external file and linked on a web page to work. It will be considered to be a part of the HTML file being parsed by the browser once it is linked.

Client and Server Side Scripting

In web development, JavaScript is termed as a client side scripting language. All the scripts that you write in

JavaScript are executed on the client side, which is your or your visitors' browser.

On the other hand, PHP and ASP are server side scripting languages. As you might have guessed, the scripts or programs created using those two are executed on the server and their results are usually sent to the client.

The two complete the concept of DHTML (Dynamic HTML). When you use client and server side scripting, your pages will become more dynamic and interactive. With them, you can create social media websites, online games, and even your own search engine. And those statements are not exaggerated. You are truly a few steps away from greatness once you master JavaScript and a server side scripting language.

However, take note that learning client side scripting is a prerequisite before learning server side scripting. After all, most of the functions and features that you will create using server side scripting will require or need the support of client side scripting. Also, client side scripting is a good introduction to programming for web developers who have no experience or even any idea on how programming works.

Before you start learning and applying JavaScript to your web documents, you should learn and master HTML and CSS. In JavaScript, you will be mostly dealing with HTML elements, so it is a requirement that you know about HTML elements and attributes.

Alternatively, if you want to use JavaScript to perform advanced styling on your document such as animations and dynamic layouts, then you should have a solid background on CSS.

To give you a short summary of the relationship between HTML, CSS, and JavaScript, take note of these pointers:

- HTML is used to define the content and elements of your web page.
- CSS is used to specify or precisely define the appearance and layout of your web page.
- JavaScript is used to create functionalities in your web page. It can also be used to define content like HTML and define appearances like CSS.

With JavaScript, you can fully control everything on your web page. You can change an HTML element's content. For example, you can change the text content of a paragraph element with JavaScript.

You can also change the value of one of the attributes of an HTML element. For example, you can change the HREF attribute of a link you inserted on your document.

And lastly, you can change the CSS or styling values of an HTML element. For example, you can change the font-weight of one of your headers in your web document with JavaScript, too.

Also, with JavaScript, you have full control on when it will be applied, unlike CSS. You can run your scripts before the page loads, while the page is loading, after the page loaded, and while your user browses the page.

On the other hand, you can make those changes automatic or triggered by the visitor. You can add other factors such as time of the day, specific user actions, or user browsing behavior to trigger those changes or functions.

Chapter 2: HTML DOM and Assigning Values

How can JavaScript do all of that? It can do all of that because it takes advantage of the HTML DOM or Document Object Model. JavaScript can access, modify, and remove any HTML element together with its properties by using HTML DOM.

Assigning Attribute Values with JavaScript

With CSS, you have dealt with selectors. By using the right selector, you can change the CSS style of a specific element, group or class of elements, group of similar elements, handpicked elements, or all of the elements in your page. By this point, you must already know how id's and classes works.

JavaScript almost works like that, too. To change the content of an element, value of an element's property or attribute, or style of an element, you will need to select them first and assign a value. Below is an example of using JavaScript to change a paragraph element's (which has a value of "testparagraph" for its id attribute) font size:

```
<head>

<script>

document.getElementById("testparagraph"
).style.fontSize = "17px";

</script>

</head>

<body>
```

```
<p  id='testparagraph'  >This  a  paragraph.
This  is  another  sentence.  This  is  the  last
sentence.</p>

</body>
```

The previous line's equivalent to CSS is:

```
#testparagraph {font-size: 17px;}
```

They have different syntax, but they will have the same result. In the CSS example, the paragraph with the "testparagraph" id was selected by placing a pound sign and typing the id value.

In JavaScript, "testparagraph" was selected using DOM. If you will translate the example JavaScript line to plain English, the line says to the browser that the line of code pertains to something or will do something within the document, which is your webpage.

Then the next part tells the browser that you are looking for a certain element that has a value of "testparagraph" on its id attribute. The next part tells the browser that you will do something to the style attribute of the "testparagraph" element. And the last part tells the browser that you will assign a value on the fontSize within the element's style attribute.

In JavaScript, the equals sign (=) means that you will assign a value to the variable or property on its left. And the value that you will assign on the variable or property is on the right.

On the example, you will assign the value "17px" to the fontSize style attribute of the element "testparagraph" that is located within your HTML document. The semicolon at the end tells the browser that it is the end of the line for that code, and it should parse the next line for it to execute.

Browser Parsing Behavior

By default, that previous JavaScript example will not work. The reason is that browsers read and execute HTML documents line by line – from the starting tag of the html tag, the browser will perform scripts, apply CSS values, place the HTML elements, place their specific contents, etcetera, until the browser reach the closing html tag.

In the example, the line asks the browser for an element that has the value "testparagraph" in its id attribute in the document. Unfortunately, the browser has not reached the body of the document where the definition of the element "testparagraph" resides.

Because of that, the browser will return an error saying that there is no element that has that attribute. You cannot assign a value for the attribute font size style to a nonexistent or null object. Hence, when the browser reaches the definition of the element "testparagraph", its font size will not be changed to the value you have set in the JavaScript code.

The solution to that is simple: you can place the script after the part where the element "testparagraph" was defined, and that is any location after the closing paragraph of the element "testparagraph".

Chapter 3: JavaScript Statements

In the last part of the previous chapter, the book loosely discussed about how browsers read HTML files and JavaScript lines and how you can assign values to an attribute. This chapter will supplement you with further discussions about that and JavaScript statements.

To construct a program using a programming language, you will need to write lines of codes. Those lines of codes are called statements. A statement is a line of code that contains an instruction for the computer to execute. In JavaScript, the one that executes the code is your internet browser.

Statements in JavaScript might contain the following: Keywords, Expressions, Operators, Comments, and Values. Below are sample lines of JavaScript that this chapter will dissect; this is done so that you will know the parts that comprise JavaScript statements:

```
var x; // This is a comment line.

var y; // To create one, you must place two
forward slashes.

var z; // Comment lines are ignored by the
browser.

x = 1 + 1; // So you can place them before
or after a statement.

y = "Hello World." // And it will not affect
the syntax.

z = 10 // But do not put them in the middle
of a statement.
```

Keywords

In the example, the word var is a keyword. Typically, keywords are reserved words that you cannot use in your program except when you need to use their purpose. In the sample statements, the keyword var tells the browser to create a variable named x. Variables will be discussed later.

Expressions

On the other hand, 1 + 1 is an expression and the + and = sign are examples of operators. Expressions, in computer programming, are combinations of operators, values, constants, and variables that will be interpreted by the computer to produce a result. In x = 1 + 1, the browser will compute or evaluate that expression and return a value of 2. Expressions are not limited to arithmetic operations in JavaScript. Expressions can be in form of Boolean comparison, string operations, and etcetera.

Values

There are two values types that you will see and use in JavaScript. The first type is fixed or literal values; the second type is variables.

Literal Values

Numbers, Strings (text enclosed in single or double quotes), and even Expressions are literal values. In the example, the parts "Hello World" (string), 10 (number), and 1 + 1 (expression) are literal values.

Variables

On the other hand, variables are data containers. Variables can contain literal values such as strings, numbers, arrays, expressions, and even objects.

To use or create one, you must name it or create an identifier for it. Identifiers are combinations of letters, underscores, and dollar signs and must not be the same with any keywords or reserved words in JavaScript.

However, take note that identifiers must start with a letter, an underscore, or a dollar sign only. Starting with a number will return an error, and including symbols other than underscores and dollar signs will not be accepted by JavaScript.

Local Variable and Global Variables

There are two types of variables in JavaScript. The first one is local and the second one is global. The type of variable depends on where it was declared. The difference between them is how they are handled in the script.

Variables that are declared outside of functions will become a global variable. And variables that are declared inside functions will become a local variable.

Global variables will stay on the memory until the web page is closed. It can be referenced and used anywhere in the script. On the other hand, local variables will only stay on the memory until the browser finishes executing the function where the variable was declared. It can be only referenced and used by the function where it was declared. Functions will be discussed later in this book.

In the sample JavaScript statements, the letters x, y, and z are global variables.

To create a variable in JavaScript, you must use the var keyword – just like in the previous example. To assign values to them, you can use the equal operator.

Operators

There are multiple of operators that you can use in JavaScript. And it can be categorized into the following:

- Arithmetic
- Assignment
- String
- Comparison
- Logical
- Conditional
- Bitwise
- Typeof
- Delete Unary +

Only the first four types of operators are mostly the ones that you will frequently use during your early days of JavaScript programming: Arithmetic, Assignment, String, and Comparison. The remaining operators are typically used for advanced projects and might be confusing for beginners.

On the other hand, take note that some of the operator symbols may serve two purposes or more. For example, the + sign can be used as an arithmetic, string, or unary + operator depending on the condition or your goal.

Comments

You might already have an idea on what comments are. As mentioned before, they are ignored by browsers, and their only function is to serve as reminders or notes for you – just like the comments in HTML. You can create a new line of comment by using two forward slashes. If you want to create a block of comment, start it with /* and end it with */.

Chapter 4: JavaScript's Basic Syntax

For the browser to execute a JavaScript statement, the statement must follow the correct syntax and must only have one instruction (this may vary depending the code).

Just a small mistake in the syntax will make the computer do something different from what you want to happen or it might not do nothing and return an error.

If you have a large block of code and one of the statements gets an error, the browser will not execute the lines that follow the statement that generated an error.

Due to that, it is important that you always check your code and avoid creating mistakes to make sure that you will achieve the things you want to happen with JavaScript.

JavaScript Syntax

JavaScript, just like other computer languages, follow syntax. In computer programming, syntax is a set of rules that you must follow when writing codes.

One of the syntax rules in JavaScript is to terminate each statement with a colon. It is like placing a dot in every sentence you make.

This rule is flexible due to ASI (Automatic Semicolon Inserting). Even if you do not place a semicolon at the end of your statement, once you start a new line, the previous line will be considered as a complete statement – as if it has a semicolon at the end. However, not placing semicolons is bad practice since it might produce bugs and errors.

Another rule is to make sure that you close brackets, parentheses, and quotations in your code. For example, leaving a dangling curly brace will result in an error. And with quotation marks, if you started with a single quote, end it with a single quote. If you start with a double quote, end with a double quote.

Take note that JavaScript is a case-sensitive language. Unlike HTML wherein you can use lower, upper, and mixed case on tags and attributes, JavaScript will return an error once you use the wrong case for a method or variable. For example, changing the capitalization of the letter b in the getElementById will result to an error.

Never create variables that have the similar name with keywords or reserved words. Also, always declare variables. If you do not explicitly declare them and use them on your statements, you might get unexpected results or a reference error. For example:

```
var y;

var z;

y = 1;

z = 1 + x;
```

Once your browser reads the last line, no value will be assigned to z because the browser will return a reference error.

That is just a few of the rules in JavaScript's syntax. Some methods and keywords follow certain syntax. Remember them to prevent yourself from the hassle of unneeded debugging.

Chapter 5: Functions and Events

You already know by now what statements are and how to write statements in accordance to JavaScript's syntax rules. You also know how to assign values to an HTML element's attribute by using JavaScript. In this chapter, you will know how to create functions or methods.

A function is a block of statements that you can call or invoke anytime to execute. In other programming languages, functions are called subroutines, methods, or procedures. The statements inside a function will not be immediately executed when the browser parses the HTML document. It will only run or be executed if it is called or invoked.

Purposes of Functions

What are the purposes of functions? First, it allows you to control when to execute a block of statements as explained previously.

Second, it allows you to create 'mini' programs in your script. For example, if you want to make a paragraph to be centered align, to have a heavier font, and to have a bigger font size when you click the paragraph, you can create a function for that goal and capture an event that will trigger that function once you click on the paragraph.

Third, creating functions is a good way to separate lengthy blocks of statements into smaller chunks. Maintaining and debugging your script will be much easier with functions.

Fourth, it can effectively lessen redundancy in your script. Instead of writing the same sequence of statements repeatedly in your script, you can just create a function, and just call it again when you need the browser to execute the statements within it once more.

Creating Functions

To create a function, you will need to use the keyword function. When you create a function you must follow a simple syntax. Below is an example of a function:

```
function MakeBolderAndBigger(elementID) {

document.getElementById(elementID).style.fon
tSize = "20px";

document.getElementById(elementID).style.fon
tWeight = "20px";

}
```

In the example, the keyword function was followed with MakeBolderAndBigger. That part is the function's name. Naming a function has the same rules with naming a variable identifier.

After the function's name, there is elementID which is enclosed in parentheses. That part of the function is called a parameter. You can place as many parameters that you want or none at all. If you place multiple parameters, you must separate them with a comma and a space. If you are not going to use parameters, just leave it blank but never forget to place the parentheses.

A parameter stores that value or the function arguments that was placed on it when the function is invoked. That parameter will act as local variable in the function. This part will be discussed further later.

Then, after the parameter, you will see a curly brace. And after the statements, there is another curly brace.

The first brace act as a sign that tells the browsers that any statements following it is a code block for the function. The second brace tells the browsers that the code block is finished, and any line of code after it is not related to the function. Those are the rules you need to follow when creating a function.

Invoking Functions

There are two common ways to invoke a function. First, you can invoke it within your script. Second, you can invoke it by placing and triggering event handlers.

Invoke within Code

The first method of invoking functions is easy. All you need to do is to type the name of the function, and fill in the arguments that the function's parameters require. To invoke the example function using the first method, you can simply type this:

```
MakeBolderAndBigger("testparagraph");
```

Once your browser reads that, it will process the function. Since you have placed "testparagraph" as the argument for the parameter elementID, elementID will have a value of "testparagraph". It will now act as a variable.

When the browser executes the first statement in the function, which is document.getElementById(elementID).style.fontSize = "20px";, it will select the element "testparagraph" and change its font size value to 20px.

On the other hand, you can actually provide no argument for function parameters. If you do this instead:

```
MakeBolderAndBigger();
```

The browser will execute the function. However, since you did not store any value to the parameter, the parameter elementID will be undefined and will have the value undefined.

Because of that, when the first statement tries to look for the element with the id attribute of elementID, which has the value of undefined, it will return an error.

Once the browser finishes executing the function, it will return on reading the next line of code after the function invocation. For example:

```
MakeBolderAndBigger("testparagraph");

document.getElementById("testparagraph").sty
le.color = "blue";
```

After the browser finishes executing the function MakeBolderAndBigger, it will proceed on executing the next statement below and make the font color of "testparagraph" to blue. The example above is the same as coding:

```
document.getElementById("testparagraph"
).style.fontSize = "20px";

document.getElementById("testparagraph"
).style.fontWeight = "20px";

document.getElementById("testparagraph"
).style.color = "blue";
```

Invoke with Events

Every action that a user does in a web page and every action that the browser performs are considered events. A few of those events are:

- When the page finishes loading

- When a user or script changes the content of a text field
- When a user click a button or an HTML element
- When a user presses on a keyboard key

To invoke a function when an event happens, you must tell the browser by placing some piece of codes in your page's HTML. Below is an example:

```
<button
onClick='MakeBolderAndBigger("testparagraph"
);' >Invoke Function</button>
```

When a user clicks on that button element, it will trigger the function MakeBolderAndBigger. The syntax for that is simple. Just insert the event inside the opening tag of an HTML element that has the event that you want to capture, place an equal sign, place the function that you want to execute together with the arguments you need to place on it, and then enclose the function in quotes.

By the way, be wary of quotes. If you used a single quote to enclose the function, then use double quotes to enclose the values on your arguments. Just think of it as if you are assigning values on an element's style attribute in HTML. Also, as best practice, never forget to place a semicolon at the end.

As a reference, below are some of the events that you can use in HTML and JavaScript:

- onClick – triggers when the user clicks on the HTML element
- onMouseOver – triggers when the user hovers on the HTML element

- onMouseOut – triggers when the user's mouse pointers move out from the element's display
- onKeyDown – triggers when the user presses a keyboard key
- onChange – triggers when the user changes the content of a text field
- onLoad – triggers when the browser is done loading the body, images, frames, and other scripts

Chapter 6: Debugging, Text Editing Tool, and References

In modern browsers, most of JavaScript errors are handled automatically and ignored to prevent browsing disruption. So when testing your scripts when opening your HTML files on a browser, it is difficult to spot errors and debug.

Web Developer Consoles on Browsers

Fortunately, a few of those browsers have built-in developer consoles where you can monitor errors and the resources that your page generates and uses. One of those browsers that have this functionality is Google Chrome. To access its developer console, you can press F12 on your keyboard while a page is open on it.

Pressing the key will open the developer tools panel within Chrome, and you can click on the Console tab to monitor the errors that your page generates. Aside from monitoring errors, you can use it to test statements, check the values of your variables, call functions, etc.

Text Editing Tool with Syntax Highlighting

You can get away with a few problems when writing HTML and CSS on typical text editing tools like Notepad. However, with JavaScript coding, using those ordinary tools is a challenge. Unlike the two, JavaScript has a strict and vast syntax. Just one typo in your script and you will start hunting bugs after you test the statements you wrote. After all, it is a programming language unlike HTML which is a markup language.

To make your life easier, it is best that you use a text editing tool with syntax highlighting when coding JavaScript. One of the best tools out there on the Web is Notepad++. It is free and it is as lightweight (in terms of resource usage) and as simple as Notepad.

The syntax highlighting will help you spot missing brackets and quotation marks. It will also prevent you from using keywords as variables since keywords are automatically highlighted in a different color, which will help you realize sooner that they are identifiers you cannot use for variables.

References

As of now, you have only learned the basics of how to code JavaScript. You might have been itching to change the values of other attributes in your HTML code, but you do not know the HTML DOM to use. On the other hand, you might be interested on knowing the other operators that you can use in your script.

The book has omitted most of them since it focused more on the coding process in JavaScript. Thankfully, you can just look up those values and operators on the net. To give you a head start, this a link to the JavaScript reference list made by the developers in the Mozilla Foundation: https://developer.mozilla.org/en-US/docs/Web/JavaScript/Reference.

Conclusion

Thank you again for purchasing this book!

I hope this book was able to help you to learn the basics of coding with JavaScript.

The next step is to:

Master the HTML DOM.

Become familiar with other keywords and their usage.

Finally, if you enjoyed this book, please take the time to share your thoughts and post a review on Amazon. We do our best to reach out to readers and provide the best value we can. Your positive review will help us achieve that. It'd be greatly appreciated!

Thank you and good luck!

Check Out My Other Books

Below you'll find some of my other popular books that are popular on Amazon and Kindle as well. Simply click on the links below to check them out. Alternatively, you can visit my author page on Amazon to see other work done by me.

C Programming Success in a Day

Android Programming in a Day

C ++ Programming Success in a Day

Python Programming in a Day

PHP Programming Professional Made Easy

CSS Programming Professional Made Easy

Windows 8 Tips for Beginners

If the links do not work, for whatever reason, you can simply search for these titles on the Amazon website to find them.

www.ingramcontent.com/pod-product-compliance
Lightning Source LLC
Chambersburg PA
CBHW070800180526
45168CB00004B/1700